THE ABCs FOR STARTING AND MANAGING YOUR OWN PUBLISHING COMPANY MADE SIMPLE

Learn how to avoid the pitfalls that prevent publishers from having a successful and profitable business

Dr. Rosie L. Milligan

Copyright © 2013 by Dr. Rosie Milligan
Los Angeles, California
All rights reserved, including the right of reproduction in whole or in part in any form.
Printed and Bound in the United States of America

Published and Distributed by:
Professional Publishing House
1425 W. Manchester Blvd., Suite B
Los Angeles, California 90047
Drrosie@aol.com
(323) 750-3592

Cover design : Jay De Vance, III
First printing : April 2013
ISBN: 978-0-9834444-2-8
Library of Congress Control Number: 2013936038

10 9 8 7 6 5 4 3 2 1

No part of this book may be reproduced, stored in a retrieval system or transmitted in any form or by any means without the prior written permission of the authors—except by a reviewer who may quote brief passages in a review to be printed in a newspaper, magazine or journal.

DEDICATION

This book is dedicated to all new publishers who choose to be successful in the publishing industry and who are willing to arm themselves with information needed to be successful and profitable.

ACKNOWLEDGMENTS

I want to acknowledge all the people who have helped me on my journey of becoming a successful and profitable publisher. I will not call names, I might forget someone. You know who you are, my staff, the editors, formatters, graphic designer, proofers, mentors, and you the readers—I truly thank you.

ABOUT THE AUTHOR

Dr. Rosie Milligan, professional business consultant, author, financial/estate planner and Ph.D. in Business Administration, has always been an achiever. Every career or business in which she has been involved includes helping others accomplish their goals in life. Her motto, "Erase No, Step Over Can't and Move Forward With Life," has been a motivating influence for hundreds to whom she has been mentor and role model.

Dr. Milligan lectures nationally on economic empowerment, management diversity in the workplace, and male/female relationships. Her books Starting a Business Made Simple and Getting out of Debt Made Simple, have helped many across the country. She is the author of seventeen books. She has co-authored four books with her sister, Attorney Clara Hunter King, What You Need To Know Before You Start A Business, Departing This Life Preparations, How To Write A Book Made Simple, and ABC's On How To Prepare Your Manuscript For Editing, Formatting, And Printing, Nuts And Bolts For The New Author and The New Publisher Made Simple, Developing A Marketing Plan For Your Book Made Simple, The ABC's For Starting And Managing Your Own Publishing Company Made Simple, and What You Need to Know Before You Get Hitched.

Dr. Milligan is an expert in the publishing industry, with thirty years experience. Under her publishing house, Professional Publishing House, she has published more than three hundred titles. Many authors she published were signed by mainstream publishers, and have taken their places on numerous best-seller's lists across the country. Using her expertise, she has set up independent publishing companies for 25 of her clients. Additionally, she assisted Maxine Thompson, a top literary agent in Southern California, launch her literary agency business.

A successful motivational speaker and trainer, she is a member of Women Speakers Association. She has appeared on numerous television and radio shows, such as Sally Jesse Raphael in New York; A.M. Philadelphia; Evening Exchange in Washington, D.C., Marilyn Kagan Show in Los Angeles, and she is a regular guest on Stevie Wonder's KJLH Radio. She is the host of a weekly live Internet talk show, "EXPRESS YOURSELF HOUR," and she is founder and director of "Black Writers on Tour."

CONTENTS

1: Choosing the Right Business Structure for Your Business 11
2: What's in a Name? 17
3: What Does the Book Title Have to do With Anything? 21
4: Why Font/Type Size Is Important 27
5: Why Your Book Interior Layout/Design Makes a Difference 31
6: Choosing a Formatter 35
7: Choosing a Graphic Designer, Illustrator 39
8: Conventional/Traditional vs. Print-on-Demand 43
9: A Website is a Must-Have 51
10: Preparing Manuscript for Editor and Formatter 55
11: The Difference Between a Copy Editor and Story Editor 61
12: Pricing Your Book for Profit 65
13: Setting Up Your Book for Lightning Source 69
14: Obtaining Your Book Credentials 73
15: Publishing Books for Other Authors 79
Appendix 83
    Publishing Contract
    Publishing Package & Book Proposal Cost
    Approval Form for the Author to Sign Prior to Book Going to the Formatter
    Approval Form for the Author to Sign Prior to Book Going to the Printer
    Formatting Change Form

1. Choosing the Right Business Structure for Your Business

Sole Proprietorship

You are the sole owner of the business. You wear all the hats; you make all the decisions and have all the responsibility and liability, as well.

Corporation

- A corporation has a chief executive officer (President), a financial officer (usually that person is the treasurer. It has a secretary and a board of directors).

- A corporation submits Articles of Incorporation to the Secretary of State and the State must approve the corporation.

- When a corporation is sued the plaintiff can only attach the assets owned by the corporation.

Partnership

- Two or more partners.

- Partners decide who will manage the business.

- Each partner has an assigned responsibility, or you may have a silent partner, one who invests money into the business, but has no input on the daily operation of the business.

- A written partnership agreement that spells out duties, responsibility and financial agreement as to how the profits will be split.

- Each partner is equally responsible for the liability of the partnership, even if he/she did not have input in the matter where an agreement or contract was entered into.

- Each partner may have their personal assets jeopardized when a judgment is placed on the partnership business.

2. What's In A Name?

The Business Name

- Is a marketing component,
- Is a branding component,
- Should signify what business you are in, and
- Should tell the public what service you provide.

For Example:

- GG's Enterprise. This name does not give any indication of the type of business you are in or the services you provide.
-
- GG's Publication. This name could suggest to some that you operate a magazine, newspaper, or other publication. However, it is not clear.
-
- GG's Publishing House. This name indicates that you are a publishing company.
- GG's Publishing. This name also indicates that you are in the publishing business.

AS YOU CAN SEE, THE NAME IS IMPORTANT!

3. What Does the Book Title Have to do With Anything?

The Book Title

- Is very important,

- Should lend itself to what the book is about, and

- Should not be misleading.

People want to know what they're purchasing, and the title will give them a clue.

Subtitles

- Sometimes, it's necessary to use a subtitle to give further clues about what your book is about. If you have the word "novel" on your front cover, it's made clear that your book is a fictional work, regardless of the title.

- For example: the book, THRIFT STORE DIVA, has a subtitle: Spending Pennies and Looking Like A Million Dollars. This sub-title helps the reader to get a clue as to what's in the book.

- The title of your book will indicate the genre: poetry, fiction, nonfiction, autobiography, self-help, a children's book, etc.

Content Assumption

Assumptive title is when a conclusion is drawn about what the book is about from the title and, in most cases, the assumption is wrong. Oftentimes a customer will not purchase the book because their assumption of what the book is about is totally incorrect. There are cases where a person has purchased a book and returned it because the title was misleading.

Examples of a Misleading Title

A CHOCOLATE GIRL IN A VANILLA WORLD

- This title will lead one to think that it is an autobiography.

- This title is a book of poetry and prose, therefore the title is misleading.

- The title should be: A CHOCOLATE GIRL IN A VANILLA WORLD: [with a subtitle] A Collection of Poetry and Prose.

"Soft" Title and "Strong" Title

- A strong title grabs the reader's attention more quickly.

- A soft title is one the reader has to look at many times before feeling compelled to pick it up.

- Soft title: "WHAT EVERY DAUGHTER NEEDS FROM HER FATHER"

- Strong title: "FATHERLESS WOMEN: [with a subtitle] What Every Daughter Needs From Her Father"

4. Why Font/Type Size is Important

Your Book Should Be Reader Friendly

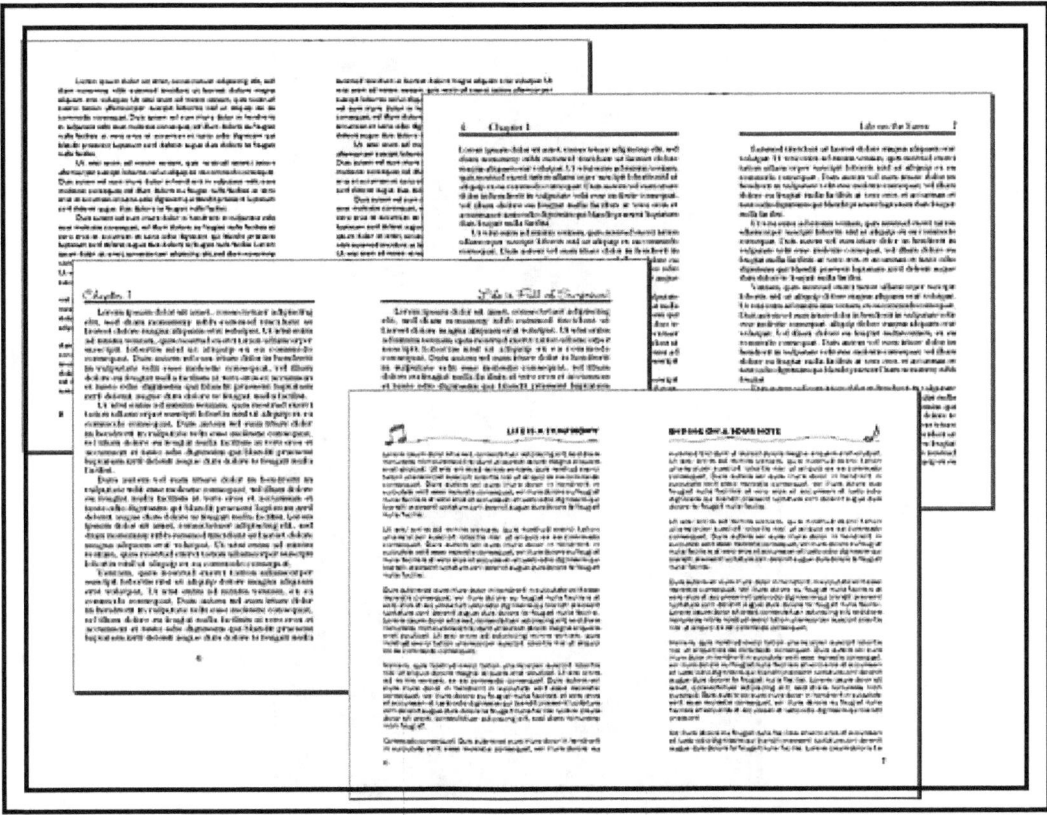

- Your book should be easy to read.

- A 12 font size is easy on the eye. Never make the font larger in order to increase your page count. Too large of a font is as hard on the eye as a font that is too small.

- Do not type your book in all capital letters.

- Do not type your book in all bold letters.

- A good, seasoned formatter can get you the page count you desire without making the font size extra large to do so.

Suggested Reading

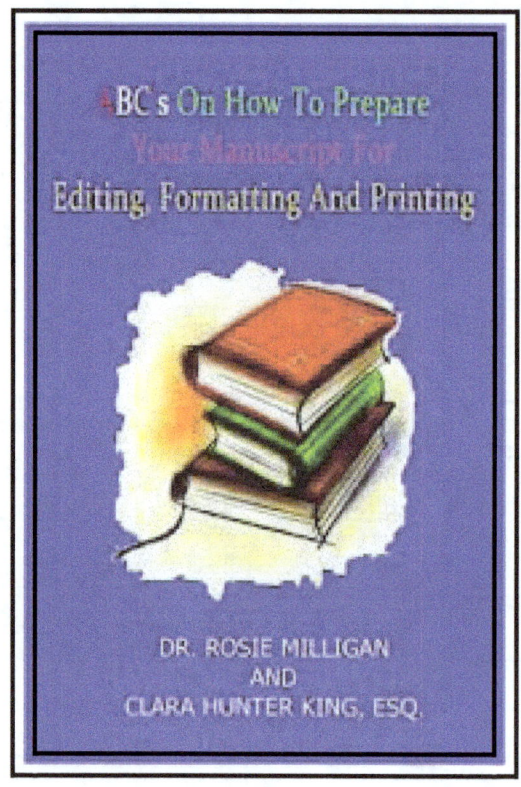

- I suggest you read a book written by me and my sister, attorney Clara Hunter King, ABC's On How To Prepare Your Book For Editing, Formatting And Printing.

5. Why Your Book Interior Layout/Design Makes a Difference

Duties of a Formatter/Designer

- Formatting your book in an appropriate style according to the genre.

- Designing a style to your book.

- Selecting a special way to introduce each new chapter, page numbers, headings, spacing, indentations/paragraphs, quotes, references, citations, footnotes/endnotes, indexes, and more

- Makes the book more attractive to the reader, easy to read and appeasing to the eye. Think of a book that you read where the text was raggedy and not justified, spacing was too close, the text was too close to the outer edge and too close to the spine of the book whereas you had to bend the cover and pages back in order to read the information near the spine.

- A good book designer/formatter makes a great difference.

6. Choosing A Formatter

How to Choose a Formatter to Design Your Book

- Many hang out their banner far too soon as a desktop publisher, book designer and for-matter.

- Some think all a formatter needs to know is how to set the margins for a book's trim size (i.e., 5.5 x 8.5, 6 x 9, etc.), learn how to make the headers and number the pages, and they think they are good to go. Wrong!

- There is much to know about professionally formatting a book.

- Different book types and genres need a special/unique look and personality. A book on finance would have a different personality than a fiction book.

- The best way to choose a formatter is by a referral from someone who has used the service and is satisfied with their work.

- The formatter should have samples of its work posted on its web site. If not, ask for samples. Furthermore, ask for a sample interior layout for your book before they begin work on your book.

- Make sure the formatter is a perfect fit for your book.

- Go to a bookstore and look at different types of books and different layouts/designs/styles.

- Purchase the book design that you like and show it to your formatter.

- When obtaining a formatter, remember that some formatters are limited in their skills. So if you plan on having text in your book to wrap around a photo, or you have graphs, charts, endnotes, index etc., you want to find out if the formatter had done this type of project before.

- You do not want your book to be a test project for the formatter.

- Find someone with the experience you need to have a professional book to present to the public.

YOUR BOOK PROJECT SHOULD REPRESENT YOU WELL.

7. Choosing a Graphic Designer, Illustrator

How to Choose the Right Graphic Designer, Illustrator

- It's always best to have a sense of what you are looking for in a book cover and for illustrations.

- It's a good idea to spend extra time with the illustrator so that you two can come to a meeting of the minds about the characters you want drawn for you book.

- Please know that if you continue to change the concept that you presented to the illustrator, he/she will have to charge you additional fees for your project.

Illustrations are charged per illustration, and each time you start over with the concept, you are asking the illustrator to create something new. If you continue doing so, each character could become a new illustration versus a modification of a character. If you are not careful, the cost for your illustrations could easily double your anticipated cost for your book project.

DO NOT EXPECT AN ILLUSTRATOR TO KEEP MAKING CHANGES AND NOT CHARGE YOU EXTRA. IT'S A LOT OF WORK INVOLVED.

8. Conventional/Traditional vs. Print-on-Demand

Conventional/Traditional Printers

Conventional/traditional printers are printers who usually print large quantity of books, and the cost is based on your print run. However, some conventional printers are now printing short-run on books also.

Short-run and print-on-demand have almost become the norm. Authors are no longer printing thousands of books and having them sit in their garages. They now create the demand for their books, and they print on demand, leveraging their finances.

When using conventional printing and major distributors order books from you, you pay the printer to print your books. When a bookstore orders from major distributors, the distributors will order the books from you. You must then ship the books to the distributor; you pay the shipping costs, and you give the distributors a 50-65% discount because they give the bookstore a 40% discount on the books they purchase from the distributor. The distributor pays the author 90 days from purchase.

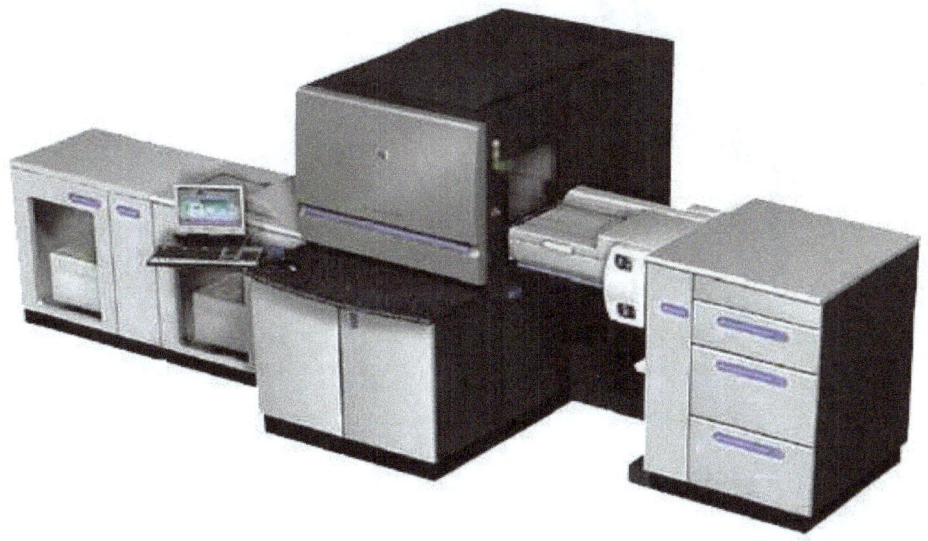

Print-On-Demand Printing

If you are set up on print-on-demand such as Lightning Source, you can order as few books as you like and the printing price is the same, unless you order 50 or more you can get 5% to 20% discount.

When bookstores order your book from the distributor, Lightning Source prints your book and the distributor (Ingram, the distributor) will ship your book to the book stores.

You give the distributor 40% discount. In 90 days, the distributor will send you a check for 40% less the retail cost, less the printing fees, and you have incurred zero shipping costs. This is a great way to print and sell your books. You are leveraging your finances; you are not paying the high cost of shipping, and you are keeping more of the money from your book in your pocket.

Book Profits
Conventional vs. Print-On-Demand

Conventional

Retail Cost	$15.00
60% Discount to Ingram Distributor	9.00
Less Printing Cost Per Book	2.50
Gross Amount Due Author	6.50
Less 20% due Professional Publishing (Dist)	1.30
Less Shipping Charge	4.50
Net Amount Due Author (Royalty)	.70*

*This does not include boxes, tape, time, etc.

Print-On-Demand

Retail Cost	$15.00
40% Discount to Booksellers/Distributors	-6.00
	9.00
Less Printing Cost Per Book	4.50
Gross Amount Due Author	4.50
Less 30% Due Professional Publishing (Dist)	1.35
Net Amount Due Author (Royalty)	$3.15

Why is Print-On-Demand Better?

When using a conventional printer, the cost per book is higher unless printing large quantities (i.e., 500 to 1,000 books). In all situations, I prefer printing with print-on-demand, because:

1. I can order 1 to 1,000 books. After placing an order, I can expect to receive my books within 7 to 10 days. The books are shipped from Tennessee via UPS Ground.

2. When a book store orders my books from Ingram Books, one of the largest book distributors, nationally and internationally. Lightning Source prints the books, whether it is one or one hundred books, Ingram will ship the book to the book seller and in 90 days they will pay the distributor (Professional Publishing House) for books sold. Ingram will deduct their 40% discount plus the printing charge and send a check for the difference to the author publisher.

3. I only have to pay up-front (out-of-pocket) for the books that I am going to sell myself. Books ordered by book store/wholesalers are printed by Lightning Source Printing, and the printing charge is deducted from my royalty statement when Ingram pays me for my books in 90 days.

Even when you order a large quantity of books from a conventional printer and get a $2.00 to 3.00 less cost per book via doing so, the bottom line in profits is extremely less.

- Ingram will order the book from the author/publisher, and they want a 60% discount on the books ordered.

- Ingram requires that the author/publisher incur the shipping charge (shipping charge is very expensive). You will incur all shipping charges, and Ingram has a return policy, books can be returned as long as the title is in print. You prepay the shipping, and you have to wait 90 days plus to get paid for your books.

- Let's say that you printed via conventional printer, and the book cost is $2.00 to $3.00 cheaper. Remember, Ingram will order the books from you/distributor and you/distributor will have to incur the shipping charge. You have to pay for the printing cost in order to have books on-hand to sell to Ingram. Even when you save $2.00 to $3.00 on printing, it will cost you more than what you saved on printing for the shipping. Shipping includes, paying for boxes or envelops to ship books in, tape, pallets to keep books from shifting, and your time for invoicing and going to the post office.

- When Amazon order books from you, they get a 55% discount, and you have to prepay the shipping charge. They pay in 60 to 90 days, and they may return books to you, too.

- When Barnes & Nobles order books from you, they get a 40% discount, and you can add the shipping charge to their invoice. They pay within 60 days. Books are shipped to the store that placed the order, and you will bill their home office.

9. A Website is a Must-Have

The Importance of Having an eCommerce Website

With the Internet, you can promote your book to book clubs, get per-mission from other sites to link to your website, or write articles for websites and mention your book as part of your byline for the article.

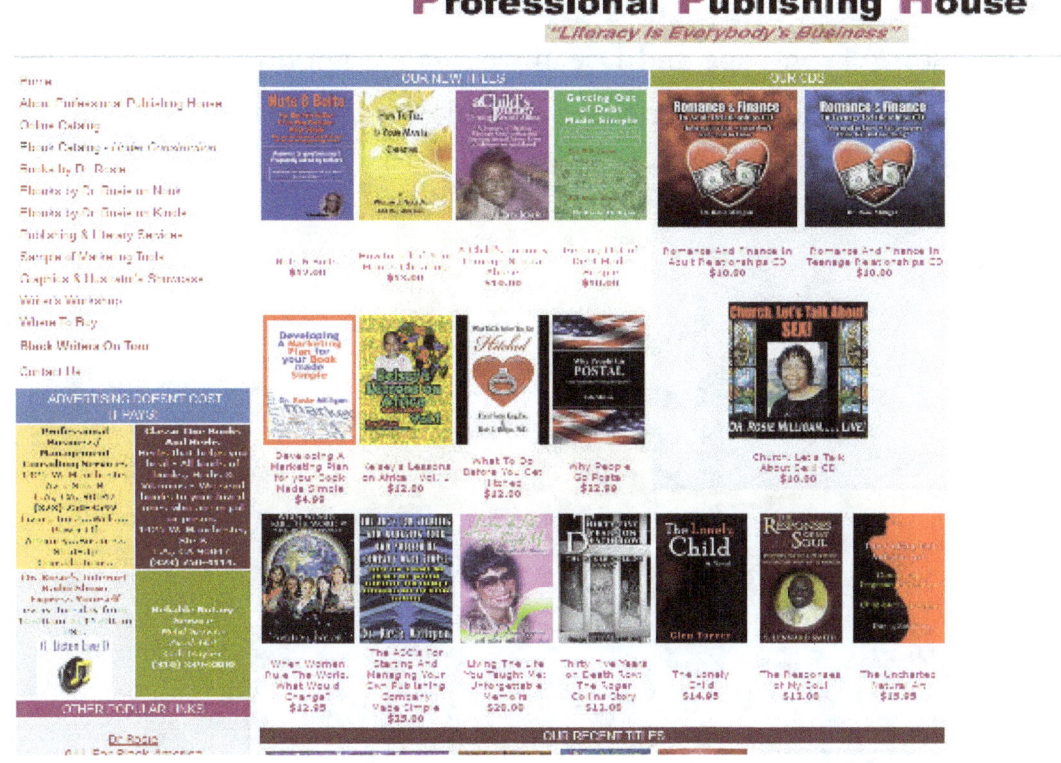

The Cost for Website Development

- You can develop an Internet and website presence for less than $60 per month. To keep costs down and control your image, you should manage your own website.

- The fee for building a basic web site should be no more than $350.00. You do not need to pay a webmaster to manage your web site. It's better to pay a web-master a consulting fee to have them teach you how to manage your site.

- Microsoft® FrontPage and Dreamweaver are good programs for building your website. With eCommerce, you make it possible for anyone to purchase your book from anywhere in the world.

10. Preparing Manuscript for Editor and Formatter

Preparing Text

1. Type your book in Microsoft® Word.

2. Use the same font throughout the whole book, preferably Times New Roman 12 pt.

3. It is important that all pages are aligned within the same margins throughout the book.

4. Start each paragraph with a left indent using the tab key.

   DO NOT USE THE SPACE BAR TO START A NEW PARAGRAPH.

5. Number each page starting with page one (1).

6. Do not press enter at the end of the line. The computer will automatically go to the next line and continue. Only press the enter key at the end of a paragraph, and this will start a new paragraph.

7. Use italics for books, movies & magazine titles.

8. Any word or sentence that you think should be emphasized, bold or italicize it.

9. If you have special prayers or scriptures that you want to be set apart in the book, italicize the selection.

10. Bold your titles and subtitles.

11. The Difference Between a Copy Editor and a Story Editor

Preparing Illustrations

Photos, artwork, line art, charts, maps, and diagrams—Your book may include one or more illustrations. It may cost extra to use illustrations, but they're almost always worth it. Some types of books (a children's book, for example) are hard to imagine without illustrations.

Preparing Photographs

If you're going to use photos that have already been developed, the original photo print is the best source for scanning. Color photos can be rendered in black and white, but not the other way around. Your computer files of photos can be used if the quality is adequate. If you take pictures with a digital camera, read the directions carefully and don't try to include photos for printing that were taken at less than 300 dpi resolution.

How to Submit Manuscripts

- One (1) printed copy of your manuscript. The text should be printed on white, 8½" x 11" ordinary bond paper. Print only on one (1) side of the paper.

- Submit the manuscript on a CD, DVD, Flash drive, or by E-mail.

Preparing Artwork

Provide original artwork, not copies, especially if it is color.

Preparing Line Art

These are drawings with no "gray scale" tones, just black lines on a white background. Send line art as "jpeg" or "TIFF" files with 300 dpi re-solutions.

Preparing Charts and Diagrams

Often your graph or chart from Word or Excel will import into the typeset program without any problem. However, illustrations must be constructed so that they will be consistent with the rest of the book.

How to Submit Manuscript to Editor and Formatter

- One (1) printed copy of your manuscript. The text should be printed on white, 8½" x 11" ordinary bond paper. Print only on one (1) side of the paper.

- Submit the manuscript on a CD, DVD, Flash drive, or by E-mail.

Tips for Easing the Page Design Process

1. Carefully label photos and artwork.

2. If you send photos or art by CD or DVD, scan photos or other art at 300 dpi resolution and send them as "jpeg" files.

3. Send original art, not art that has been printed.

Copy Editor

The copy editor is mainly concerned with spelling, grammar, and sentence structure. This editor makes certain that all of your words are spelled correctly and that there is subject and verb agreement throughout the story. A good copy editor checks for sentence fragments, run-on sentences, or paragraphs that are too long, as well as makes sure that adjectives and adverbs are used sparingly and correctly.

Story Editor

The story editor is concerned with things such as: pacing (Does the story move along well? Does the reader have to reread to make sense of what is happening in the story?); character development (Can the reader connect with or "feel" the characters? Are the characters believable?).

The story editor is also concerned with whether you are introducing too many characters at the same time; conflict (Is conflict or tension introduced early enough in the story? Does the reader get a sense of tension building, and is the reader motivated to keep reading to see the resolution?); verb tense consistency (Is the writer consistent in the use of the present or past tense?); point of view (Is the story told in the first or the third person? Is the story being told by the writer, a narrator, or the main character?).

A good story editor will help you use the art of Show vs. Tell. Do you have language dissonance regarding the type of characters that you are portraying? For example, do you have a scientist speaking in street talk, or a street person speaking like a college professor? If you do, there should be a logical reason, such as the scientist who has pulled himself up by his bootstraps from the streets, or the street person who has self-educated himself. Do you plant a "MacGuffin"—which is a goal or desire or yearning, which will fuel the plot?

Are you telling the reader or are you showing the reader the drama? Can the reader feel what is happening? Does the reader get caught up in the story? Are you involving the emotions of your reader so that he/she will root for your main character? Are you using a compelling situation? Have you layered your plot and your subplots? Do you use stilted versus conversational dialogue? Do you introduce your back story too soon?

This is only the beginning. There is much more to what a story editor looks for when editing a novel, but the input of such a professional is incalculably valuable to any writer, whether it is their first novel or their tenth.

12. Pricing Your Book for Profit

Pricing Your Book

Here are a few pointers for pricing your book for profit. Number one is that you cannot base you price on how much research and time you put into your book—the reader is not concerned about that and could care less.

1. You should go to bookstores and compare books that are similar to your book in genre and page count. I does not matter to the reader that you can only print a few copies and therefore your printing price is very expensive and therefore you have to charge more to make a profit, again, the reader could care less about that.

2. When pricing your book you must consider the cost of printing, so search for the best professional printer. Take into consideration the distributions that you are going to utilize for distributing your books. Examine the discount each distributor expects from you such Ingram wants 60% discount with a return policy and with you paying the shipping cost when shipping them your books. Amazon.com requires a 55% discount; you have to pay for shipping to them with a return policy. When selling to bookstores including Barnes and Noble bookstores a 40% discount is required, they will pay for shipping.

3. When your books are printed by Ingram, you are able to select the discount you want to offer and you can choose to not accept returns. Remember, when a book store orders your books from Ingram Books, if Lightning Source prints your books, then Ingram ships the books to the bookstore, you do not incur the shipping charge. Lightning Source will pay you in 90

days, they will deduct from the retail price the percentage of discount that you offer them and the printing cost and they will send you the balance.

4. When a retail customer orders your book you are getting paid the retail cost and the customers are paying the shipping cost.. When counting the cost of shipping consider, envelopes, boxes, labels, tape and pellets to pack the book with.

5. When pricing consider that you are not a celebrity writer and you are not a national known writer. So don't try to make a living off of just one book. You can get there but it takes time.

6. When pricing your book consider that the retailer, sales tax is added to the book cost and shipping cost. Therefore would you rather make $5.00 per book from the sale of 1,000 books or $7-10 dollars for the sales from 200 books?

13. Setting Up Your Book for Lightning Source, Inc.

About Lightning Source, Inc.

Lightning Source, Inc. is connected with Ingram Book Group, the largest book distributor in the U.S.A., as well as internationally. Once your book is set up with Lightning Source, it is placed on Amazon.com and Barnes and Nobles.com web sites.

Questionnaire for Publishers with Answers to Questionnaire

Once you have successfully completed your application and have received your approval email from Lightning Source with your Username and Password, you can log on and go to **How to Set up Your Title, How to Upload Your Files** and **How To Place An Order**. Just follow the steps for these procedures—they are simple instructions—now you are ready, set, on your mark, let's go.

14. Obtaining Your Book Credentials

How To Order Your ISBN Numbers

- Log on to www.myidentifiers.com

- Click on the Register Button on the upper right hand side of the webpage.

- Fill out the page as instructed.

- After you register with My Identifiers, choose a username and password.

- Then, you can place your order for the number of ISBNs you want.

    - 1 ISBN for $125.00

    - 10 ISBNs for $250.00

- Please remember your username and password.

- If you have any questions on how to set up your account, call 1-888-269-5372

How To Add Your Book With
My Identifiers.com (Books In Print)

What is MyIdentifiers.com?

MyIdentifiers.com provides publishers with tools and resources to purchase and assign book identifiers such as ISBNs, SANs, DOIs and others available through Identifier Services. MyIdentifiers.com provides a host of discover-ability services and solutions for publishers including automated tools to update or add to their title listings in Bowker's Books In Print and Global Books In Print databases.

Why should I register with MyIdentifiers.com?

MyIdentifiers.com allows you to easily organize, communicate and market your book titles and optimize their discovery among a wide audience of book, audio and video buyers. Bowker is the leading provider of bibliographic data and your titles are exposed to many facets of the book industry through this single web application.

Once you find the right titles, Books in Print offers professional and patron list management tools to save titles and streamline workflows. Connect—find favorite authors, genres, and purchase points Books In Print is used every day by thousands of book professionals and library patrons to make connections: connecting you to favorite authors and series; connecting genres.

1. Log On to www.myidentifiers.com
2. Click On, My Company link on the upper right hand corner of the page
3. On My Company Page, Click On Manage ISBNs Button
4. Then, Click on Assign Title Link
5. Follow These 4 Steps Below and Complete Each Section
    a. Title & Cover
    b. Contributors (Authors)
    c. Format & Size
    d. Sales & Pricing

How To Register Your Copyright

1. Log on to www.copyright.gov
2. On The Homepage, Look Under How To Register A Work
3. Then, Log on to eCO link
4. Click On, under Click Here To Register link at the bottom of the left hand page
5. Complete The Application Form
6. Log on to www.copyright.gov
7. Online signup is $35.00, Register Through Mail is $65.00
8. Click on Register a Claim on the left hand side of the page,
9. Follow Steps 1,2, and 3
10. Click The Start Registration Button
11. Click on Type of Work Button at the bottom of the Page and Select Literary Work
12. Note. Do not pre-register your work. This does not apply to you.
13. Do not click on Special Handling Section. There is a $760.00 charge
14. Click on Save For Later Button to save your information until you are ready to Pay for the Copyright

Dr. Rosie L. Milligan

Instructions for Applying to the Library Of Congress

1. Log on to www.loc.gov/publish/pcn

2. To Open up an account Click on Open An Account underneath Electronic PCN

3. Click on The Application to Participate link below the page

4. Complete the Application as Instructed

5. Once You Sign Up With The Library of Congress, Then keep your username and password for safe keeping.

6. Log on to www.loc.gov/publish/pcn

7. Click on Login link Then put in your username and password

8. Click on PCN Application On Main Menu Page

9. Fill out your Information As Required

15. Publishing Books for Other Authors

Food for Thought...

1. Prepare a publishing contract. (See Appendix for a sample contract.)

2. Prepare a book proposal cost contract and have the author to sign it. (See Appendix for sample book proposal.)

3. You should choose the editor, because the end result will reflect on your company. (It's a good idea to hire a proofreader to proof the book after the editor has finished. We all can have an oversight when editing. Include $1.00-$1.50 per page for a proofreader. Make sure this is not the proofreader's first job. Get a referral.

4. After the book has been edited and proofread, have the author reread the manuscript. Have the author sign a form stating that he/she has read the edited manuscript and approved its readiness to go to the formatter. This is important because authors, many times, seem to never finish writing their book, they want to add and make changes after the book has been formatter, changes could change the page pagination which could result in extra charges. (I have attached a form for the author to sign in the appendix)

5. When you get back the galleys (proof pages of the finished book), read with the eye of an eagle before sending to the printer. Make sure the author clearly marks any corrections he/she wants, using accepted proofreader's marks and a red pen. This is the appropriate time for the author to ensure his/her message is being conveyed or if a word has been dropped, etc. However, do keep in mind that authors are so anxious to get that book "baby" in their hand they will rush through reading the galleys.

6. As the publisher, you should explain the importance of taking the extra time and reading their book, because in the end, the content will reflect positively or poorly on the author. But, this is not the time to add additional content and rewrite the book. Corrections are one thing and rewriting is another. There will be an extra charge when rewriting your book after the book has been formatted. In fact, the book should go back to the editor when there are major changes and rewrites, before sending back to the formatter. (See Appendix for Author Approval form.)

7. When you get back the galleys (proof pages of the finished book), read with the eye of an eagle before sending to the printer. Make sure the author clearly marks any corrections he/she wants, using accepted proofreader's marks and a red pen. This is the appropriate time for the author to ensure his/her message is being conveyed or if a word has been dropped, etc. However, do keep in mind that authors are so anxious to get that book "baby" in their hand they will rush through reading the galleys.

I have included in the appendix a formatting change form. This form was developed by one of my editors/ formatter: TWA Solutions. I adapted the form for use when an author has changes after the book has been formatted. This form tends to force the author to provide clarification as to the changes to be made that has resulted from an error and not an after-thought for rewriting.

There is always a chance that any business can have a lawsuit brought against them, therefore you want to protect yourself via a paper trail, that' is the reason for having the authors to sign the forms I have placed in the appendix.

Appendix

Publishing Contract

JACK SPRAT PUBLISHING

1796 W. Cedar Avenue,– Los Angeles, CA 90047
Telephone: (323) 689-2222 · Fax: (323) 751.9988
www.jackspratpublishing.org · cedar@aol.com

AGREEMENT FOR PROFESSIONAL PUBLISHING SERVICES
Between

JACK SPRAT PUBLISHING

And

JANE DOE

This Agreement is made and entered into this --- day of -------- by and between JACK SPRATT PUBLISHING, hereinafter referred to as "PUBLISHER," and JANE DOE, hereinafter referred to as "AUTHOR(S

Witnesseth

Whereas, AUTHOR(S) desires to engage PUBLISHER to publish and distribute a book entitled, "My Journey Back" Hereinafter, referred to as "THE BOOK."

Now therefore, PUBLISHER and AUTHOR(S) for a consideration and under terms and conditions of this Agreement as set forth below do mutually agree as follows:

I. DEFINITIONS

    A.   Publisher - For purposes of this Agreement, PUBLISHER is JACK SPRATT PUBLISHING

    B.   Author(s) - For purposes of this Agreement, JANE DOE, is the writer and owner of the manuscript

    C.   Book - For purposes of this Agreement, THE BOOK is a completed manuscript or completed book (circle one; AUTHOR(S) must initial choice).

    D.   CD/Flash Drive/Electronic File - For purposes of this Agreement, is the manuscript in its completed form, including, but not limited to Table of Contents and Bibliography.

E. Publishing – For purpose of this Agreement, "publishing" shall mean presentation of THE BOOK to the public. Publishing shall include, but not be limited to distribution and packaging.

F. Distribution - For purposes of this Agreement, "distribution" shall mean to make the best effort to sell THE BOOK to wholesalers and bookstores.

G. Packaging - For purposes of this Agreement, "packaging" shall mean PUBLISHER shall engage in the following activities to assist AUTHOR(S) to build or rebuild THE BOOK.

1. Review manuscript or completed copy of THE BOOK;
2. Advise or recommend to AUTHOR(S) necessary changes in text, formatting, design of cover or other illustrations in THE BOOK and/or on a CD/Electronic File presented by AUTHOR(S) to PUBLISHER.
3. Upon completion of editing the book, PUBLISH will deliver to AUTHOR(S) the edited manuscript via email/hard copy. AUTHOR(S) shall make all changes and return to PUBLISHER. Once the AUTHOR(S) have made all changes to the manuscript, the manuscript is ready for formatting.
4. The manuscript is then presented to the formatter for formatting. Upon completion of formatting of the book, the book is sent to the AUTHOR(S) for written approval for printing prior to presentation to printer (Any page additions or page changes made to manuscript at this point, after formatting is completed, will be billed at the usual per page rate for formatting.)
5. Advise and recommend to AUTHOR(S) changes in design of cover of THE BOOK to enhance marketability and sales;
6. Advise AUTHOR(S) where necessary regarding choice of paper stock, size of print run and pricing;
7. Cause THE BOOK to be printed by presenting THE BOOK to such printing business known to PUBLISHER to be timely, dependable to keep deadlines, reliable and trustworthy for quality printing service;
8. THE BOOK shall be published under the name of JACK SPRATT PUBLISHING. Author may elect to change to her own publishing company if she wishes to.
9. ...and such other activities as may be added by amendments
10. AUTHOR(S) and PUBLISHER shall engage in at least the following activities to complete packaging THE BOOK (Place appropriate initials below.);
    a. Copyright shall be obtained by:
       CP   or   AUTHOR(S) ____CP_____
       Initials   Initials
    b. ISBN (International Standard Book Number) shall be obtained by:
       CP   or   AUTHOR(S) ____CP_____
       Initials   Initials
    c. Bar Code shall be obtained by:
       CP or   AUTHOR(S) _____CP_____
       Initials   Initials

H. **Shipping** - For purposes of this Agreement, "shipping" shall mean causing THE BOOK and/or relevant materials to be delivered for sale to destinations by the United States Postal Service, Express Mail, courier service, United Parcel Service (UPS) and any such reputable transportation or freight carrier.

I. **Copyright** - For purposes of this Agreement, "copyright" shall mean registering THE BOOK with the Library of Congress to protect and safeguard all privileges, rights and ownership of THE BOOK.

J. **ISBN (International Standard Book Number)** - For purposes of this Agreement, "ISBN" shall mean a number assigned to THE BOOK by an authorized legal agency to identify THE BOOK.

K. **Bar Code** - For purposes of this Agreement, "bar code" shall mean the standard vertical markings encoded with price of THE BOOK and other information to identify THE BOOK.

L. **Graphic Design** - For purposes of this Agreement, "graphic design" shall mean artistically rendered visual impressions on the cover of THE BOOK and/or contained within THE BOOK as illustrations.

M. **Editing** - For purposes of this Agreement, "editing" shall mean amending text and/or graphic design of THE BOOK, manuscript and/or CD.

N. **Proofing** - For purposes of this Agreement, "proofing" shall mean review of text and graphic design to detect grammatical, structural, esthetical, and/or other errors in text or graphic design.

O. **Printing** - For purposes of this Agreement, "printing" shall mean an act by JACK SPRATT PUBLISHING that shall cause THE BOOK to be presented to such printing business to be duplicated in a quantity specified by the publisher. JACK SPRATT PUBLISHING shall use best efforts to use only such printing business known to be timely, dependable to keep deadlines, reliable, and trustworthy to provide quality printing service.

P. **Formatting** - For purposes of this Agreement, "formatting" shall mean the act of creating style for THE BOOK from a CD/Electronic File and determining dimensions as part of packaging to make THE BOOK print ready.

Q. **Packaging Fee** - For purposes of this Agreement, "packaging fee" shall mean the amount of money charged to AUTHOR(S) by PUBLISHER to produce THE BOOK in a finished, marketable format.

R. **Estimated Cost of Professional Product** - For purposes of this Agreement, the "Estimated Cost of Professional Product" is a document which is incorporated by reference to this Agreement and attached hereto. Said document provides specified costs of packaging and other relevant services as information to AUTHOR(S). Said document is not intended to represent the total cost of "packaging" THE BOOK, unless expressly stated on the face of said document.

II. TERM OF AGREEMENT

This Agreement shall continue in full force and effect unless or until canceled, by (1) conduct of either party to this agreement that shall constitute a <u>breach</u> of terms, failure of conditions, non-performance or failure to perform duties as set forth herein; or (2) at the election of Author, upon <u>ten (10) days prior written notice to PUBLISHER that Author has obtained</u> a fully executed contract from a publishing house or literary agent. <u>In the event of cancellation pursuant to option (2), the return of books remaining in Publisher's possession, as well as the payment of shipping charges and the disposition of accounts receivable, shall be as described in paragraph X below.</u>

III. SCOPE OF SERVICES AND AGREEMENT

    A.   PUBLISHER agrees to provide the following services to AUTHOR(S):

1. To cause THE BOOK to be printed in a professional manner and such manner shall be reasonably acceptable to AUTHOR(S) indicated by written approval of formatted book and cover design prior to printing.
2. To cause THE BOOK to be printed in a timely manner as set forth below.
3. To provide reasonable and necessary consulting services to AUTHOR(S) directly or by competent designee acting as agent of PUBLISHER during term of this Agreement. Such consultation shall be done by United States mail, facsimile transmission, telephone, overnight (Express Mail), courier service, e-mail, or some such similar means when necessary to meet deadlines consistent with terms of this Agreement.

PUBLISHER shall notify AUTHOR(S) in writing or in a reasonably acceptable manner, if and when costs of above consultation become excessive.

    B.   AUTHOR(S) agrees to provide the following to PUBLISHER:

A consistently maintained and open line of communication to assure accuracy for and during the development of THE BOOK.

IV. PARTNERSHIP AND COMPENSATION

A. Copyright

AUTHOR(S) and PUBLISHER agree that this undertaking is a partnership with both parties bringing necessary talents together to complete a work. And because of this unique relationship, both AUTHOR(S) and PUBLISHER shall collaborate as a team — but with **copyright ownership belonging to AUTHOR(S).**

B. Payment and Financial Matters

1. Payments to PUBLISHER

For purposes of compensation to PUBLISHER, AUTHOR(S) agrees to provide up-front costs of the project, based upon the quoted prices provided by PUBLISHER on -------

2. **Payment Schedule**

   All fees are payable in advance, except printing costs. Printing costs shall be paid upon submission to printer.

3. **Revenue Sharing and Distribution**

   PUBLISHER and AUTHOR(S) agree that AUTHOR(S) shall receive all revenue derived from sales, less the following payments to PUBLISHER:

   -- percent of sales to major distributors (

   -- percent of book sales to small, independent distributors

   ---percent of book sales to bookstores who purchase books directly from PUBLISHER.

   -- of net sales for payment on books sold via print-on-demand (Ingram via Lightning Source Printing)

4. **Billing and Collection**

   PUBLISHER agrees to handle all billing and collection of sales and receipts, with the understanding that PUBLISHER will notify AUTHOR(S) of the status of any and all books that have been shipped to distributors, booksellers, media or other entities or parties. Further, on no later than the 15th calendar day of each month, following a 90 day cycle, PUBLISHER shall mail via United States Postal Service or an express mail service for overnight delivery, payment of any and all compensation due and earned by AUTHOR(S) for the preceding months along with a written statement of all book sales, shipping cost, books returned and professional fees charged.

5. After 90 days of being unable to collect, with the consent of AUTHOR(S), PUBLISHER will turn account over to a collection agency, fee to be paid by AUTHOR(S).

IV ASSIGNABILITY

PUBLISHER shall not assign any interest in this contract, and shall not transfer any interest in the same without prior written consent of the AUTHOR(S).

V. INDEMNIFICATION

AUTHOR(S) shall indemnify and save PUBLISHER harmless against any and all claims, demands, suits or payments of sums of money to any party accruing against AUTHOR(S) for injury or damage growing out of and/or resulting from the information in the book, while PUBLISHER is engaged in or about or in connection with the discharge of performance of PUBLISHER'S obligation under this Agreement.

VI. REMEDIES

All remedies and resolutions of disputes accorded herein or otherwise available to any party hereto by operation of law shall be cumulative, and no one such remedy shall be exclusive of any other. Any claim or dispute arising out of this Agreement shall be determined by arbitration, conducted under the then-prevailing rules of the American Arbitration Association in the State of California. The award of the arbitrator may be entered for judgment in any court having jurisdiction. The arbitrator may award reasonable attorney's fees to the prevailing party. This agreement shall be construed and the legal relations between the parties determined in accordance with the laws of the State of California.

VII. NOTICES AND PAYMENTS

To AUTHOR(S): All notices from PUBLISHER to AUTHOR(S) may be given in writing by mailing the notice to AUTHOR(S) by registered or certified mail, postage prepaid, or by overnight delivery service, signature required and postage prepaid, or via e-mail; or at PUBLISHER'S option, PUBLISHER may deliver such notice to AUTHOR(S) personally. The date of mailing or of personal delivery shall be deemed to be the date of service. If the deadline for notice hereunder falls on a weekend or legal holiday, then notice shall be timely if given on the next business day. Payments and notices to AUTHOR(S) shall be sent to AUTHOR(S) at: 777 Westchin Blvd, Los Angeles, Ca, or can be sent to Jane Doe @ yahoo.com

To PUBLISHER: All notices from AUTHOR(S) to PUBLISHER shall be given in writing by registered or certified mail, postage prepaid, or by overnight delivery service, signature required and postage prepaid, or by messenger, addressed as PUBLISHER 1111 Cedar Avenue, Los Angeles, CA. For e-mail, notices can be sent to *Cedar* P @yahoo.com

VIII. SEVERABILITY

Nothing contained herein shall require the commission of any act or the payment of any compensation which is contrary to law. If there shall exist any conflict between this Agreement and any such law, the latter shall prevail; and the provision or provisions hereof affected shall be curtailed, limited or eliminated to the extent (but only to the extent) necessary to remove such conflict; and as so modified, this Agreement shall continue in full force and effect. IX. AGREEMENT TERMS CONFIDENTIAL

The parties agree that they will not voluntarily publish, publicly disclose or disclose in a manner which will reasonably lead to publication of the terms or provisions of the Agreement, including specifically those relating to compensation.

IX. CANCELLATION

Only, if either party of this Agreement fails to fully and faithfully execute their respective responsibilities and agreements of terms and conditions, the other party can terminate the contract by written notice of said intention at least thirty (30) days prior to date of said termination. All books remaining in PUBLISHER'S possession will be returned to AUTHOR(S). Shipping charges will be paid by AUTHOR(S). Monies collected from outstanding accounts receivable will be processed as outlined in IV.B.3. For the consideration and under the conditions set forth above, PUBLISHER has agreed to perform the specified services for AUTHOR. Jane Doe, 1111 Hill Street, Los Angeles, CA 90016.email Janed@gmail.com

-

_____   _____
Date   JACK SPRAT PUBLISHING

_____   _____
Date   Author's Signature

_____   _____
Date   Author's Signature

Publishing Package & Book Proposal Cost

XXXXXXX Publishing House.

142 W. Cisley Avenue, Suite "D," Los Angeles, CA 90010
Telephone: (323) XXX -XXXX Fax: (323) XXX-XXXX
www.XXXXXpublishinghouse.com · XXXX@aol.com

March 16, 2013

Dear John Doe:

Thank you for your inquiry to XXXX Publishing House, XXXX Publishing House offers consulting/packaging services. We help authors set up their own publishing company for a fee.

Our objective at XXXXX Publishing House is to provide a solution to the impossible task many new authors face when trying to get their first work published. The number of new books entering the market each year makes it extremely difficult for a new author to be picked up by a large publishing house. With this in mind, XXXX Publishing House has developed a program which assists selected new authors in getting their books published and noticed in the market place—and finally noticed by the large publishers. Once a book is accepted under this program, XXXX Publishing House will assist the author in publishing their book by creating their own publishing company. We also publish books for authors under our company. All costs and schedules are attached.
(See Book Proposal Cost on page 2).

Attached is an outline of the XXXX Publishing House Publishing Program for your review. After you have reviewed the Book Proposal Cost if you are interested in pursuing this publishing option, please let us know.

We look forward to hearing from you and wish you much success with your writing project.

Sincerely,

John Doe

Book Proposal Cost

XXXX Publishing House will assist a new author in bringing their publishing project from concept to market by assisting the author to develop their own publishing company as well as assist in the marketing and distribution of the book. XXXX Publishing House also publishes authors' books.

Packaging system contains three parts:

- Development - bringing the book from the author's concept to a finished product with complete book credentials and market ready for sales in the store.

- Marketing - getting the book prepared is only 50% of the project. Once the book is complete, two things must happen: distribution and marketing. Distribution is the most difficult thing for a new author to achieve. Additionally, XXXX Publishing House will assist in creating consumer demand.

- Consulting - XXXX Publishing House will provide the Development and Marketing expertise, as well as, secure distribution with the largest national book distributor—Ingram Books.

DEVELOPMENT

ISBN# ($125.00 for one ISBN # and $259.00 for 10 numbers)	125.00
Barcode	30.00
Copyright (30.00 when obtained online and 65.00 when mailing book)	30.00
Graphic Design (cover of book)	
Editing ($XXX per page)	
Formatting ($XXX per page)	
*Consulting/Packaging Fee	$XXXXX
*(See Explanation on page 3)	
TOTAL PREPRINTING COST	$XXXXXX

Note: These fees do not include "Printing Cost." Printing costs are extra and is based on number of pages, photo scanning, retouch, and quantity. XXXX Publishing House will assist you in achieving the best price. (Illustrations for children books are quoted per project)

Formatting charges are more per page when the book requires tables, boxes, illustrations, complex designs.

*CONSULTING /PACKAGING

Development:

- Bringing the book from the author's concept to a finished product with complete book credentials and market ready.

Marketing:

- Taking the product from product to market:
- Develop press release.
- Develop media/press package.

- Place book on XXXXXXXXX PublishingHouse.com, Amazon.com, and Barnes&Noble.com.
- Set your company up with Lightning Source Printing Co. Your book will then be made available on *i-page*, a site for book stores and libraries to purchase on-line from Ingram. They have a password for Ingram's site. They are able to view the front cover of your book and all pertinent information.
- Develop your press kit which includes your Press Release and About the Author.
- Help you in setting up your book unveiling celebration.
- Provide you with a new author's package which include: a goal sheet for 6-months, 12-months, and 2-years, and suggest activities that will help you to achieve your goals.

Additionally, it is important to note that if the author makes any changes to the book after it has been formatted,(book has been laid out for printing) the author will be charged additional formatting fees. NOTE: If you change even one sentence on a page, many other pages may need reformatting as well. When you make changes, after your book has been formatted completely, the second formatting is considered a new job and priced on a per page basis.

_____   _____
Author's Signature   Date

_____   _____
XXXXXXXXXX House Representative's Signature   Date

Publishing Payment Schedule

XXXXXXXXX Publishing House has a motto of making publishing affordable. If you take a survey of current publishing rates you will find ours more than fair and quite competitive. By using the following schedule, we are able to allow our writers to get their books published at their own pace. Please refer to your *Book Proposal Cost* sheet for details.

> Step 1: To begin the book project we require 100% of the packaging, consulting and editing fees. If the book is fictional it may require story editing. In that instance, story editing is done prior to copyediting.

> Step 2: After your approval of story editing (if applicable) and copyediting changes, our book is ready for formatting (preparing and designing your text to be printed). You are required to pay 50% of the formatting fee to start the process. The balance is due upon completion.

> Step 3: The cover design can be done simultaneously with either Step 1 or Step 2, or it may be done separately. You are required to pay 50% of the cover design fee to begin this process. The balance is due upon completion.

> Step 4: When you are ready to have your book printed, all printing cost must be paid prior to your book being submitted to the printer. It takes 5-10 days to receive a printed proof of your book, after you have approved the proof; it takes approx 7-10 days for you to receive your printed book order. (It takes a little longer for a hard copy with a flap jacket)

If you would like to discuss in more detail how XXXXXXX Publishing House can fulfill your publishing needs, please contact me at (323) XXX – XXXX.

Sincerely,

John Doe

Approval Form for the Author to Sign Prior to Book Going to the Formatter

Formatting Approval Agreement

I,_____ have carefully read my manuscript. I approve my manuscript for formatting.

Additionally, it is important to note that if the author makes any changes to the book after it has been formatted, the author will be charged additional formatting fees. NOTE: If you make changes, many other pages may need reformatting as well. When you make changes, to your book after it has been formatted, you will be charged on a <u>per page</u> basis. If you make changes such as deleting pages, adding pages and any other major changes, you will be charged at an hourly rate, and fees must be paid prior to formatter starting the work. You must submit a formatting change form to the publisher.

_____   _____
Author's Signature   Date

_____   _____
Publisher Representative's Signature   Date

Special Notice! The author must make payment in advance for any correction(s)/additions(s) to be made to the book.

Approval Form for Author to Sign Prior to Book Going to Printing

Book Printing Agreement

I, _____ have carefully read my manuscript that has been formatted and made print ready. I approve the book for printing.

_____   _____
Author's Signature   Date

_____   _____
Publisher Representative's Signature   Date

Note: The publisher will not be liable for any future corrections/additions once the book has been approved. The author will have to pay for any costs associated with any future corrections or additions.

Special Notice! The author must make payment in advance for any correction(s)/additions(s) to the book.

Formatting Change Form

TWA SOLUTIONS

Changes Forms

Date: _____
Title of Manuscript: _____
Author's Name: _____

Note: The text in RED shows an example of how to indicate changes/deletions.

Page #	Paragraph #	Line #	Change From	Change To
15	5	6	Schedule everyone, please.	Schedule everyone for the same time, please.
Dedication	2	3	John Doe.	John Doe and Mary John.
17	6	2	Where is he going?	Italicize
215	3	2	The massage was simply marvelous!	Delete
— BEGIN MAKING CHANGES/DELETION BELOW —				

www.ingramcontent.com/pod-product-compliance
Lightning Source LLC
Chambersburg PA
CBHW082052230426
43670CB00016B/2868